For

w/ affectionate regret

— David

10.14.18

POROUS BORDERS

DAVID GIANNINI

Spuyten Duyvil
New York City

ACKNOWLEDGEMENTS

Chroma, "Minimalist" and "Inanimate Desire."
Country Valley Press, "Elegy," "In Sedona."
Defenestration.net "Theatre Star" (*Flash Suite* Finalist Award, 2015.)
Litter, "Alibi"; "The Archaeologist Speaks to Her Intern." (formerly called "Archao-logical.")
Merde, "Shift Thing, An Assay" and *"B.S."*
Posit Journal, #6, "So-Called."
Pushing the Envelope: Epistolary Poems [Anthology]: "Quotes, a Collaged Letter."
Up the River, "Something Else."
In limited edition chapbooks from *The Feral Press / Prehensile Pencil Publications*):
When We Savor What Is Simply There: "Earth Day;" "Myth Of Ferns."
Inverse Mirror "Regarding Scissors."
Sunlight As A Little Foe: "Squeeze-Box;" "Cabinets;" "Shutters;"
Raven Pillow & Time: "Raven;" "Pillow & Time."
In A Limited Edition Chapbook From Country Valley Press:
Four Plus Four (Chapbook), "Valentine."

Library of Congress Catalonging-In-Publication Data applied for.

FOR PAM
AND TO MARK FARRINGTON

Contents

Porous Borders

As Preface

He first met Porous Borders, considered insane by some, a tutelary spirit by others, while looking over some of his own poems that seemed not rightly achieved. He had either forced the poems to become excessively compressed, or else they were in need of more detail and flexibility of the sort found in most manners of prose.

Throughout the years he found another place, also of poetry, a place of lyric dissociation, a locus wherein processes askew to the usual, quotidian, state of mind make their own events occasioned by smuggling the invisible over the borders of normative prose and allowing them to stand as micro-monoliths, as vertical prosepoems.

Porous Borders showed the way.

Oh, but let's not become too abstract and away from the body, from sensual, lip-smacking perceptions, says Porous. Let's also get sexy. Somebody toss him an apple or a fig! How about a kiss, or a rock? Ah, to avail of invariance, like a rock, there's a thought. Relative to rock, what of spit and metaphysics is not mere dalliance? Put it this way: less cannot be said, more cannot be said: I am Porous Borders in his head.

SHUTTERS

Inside this room, I open the shutters only to find another set of shutters in back of them. I open those, then find yet another pair, open them, then another and another to open until finally there is a man who looks exactly like me standing outside the last pair of shutters. Narcissus? I ask. No, Porous, he says. And he starts stepping in past the outermost shutters, then passes the next pair, then the next and the next until his nose is touching mine as if each of us pressed up against a mirror, or each is a shutter for the other, the inner and the outer man allowing a little shade, a little sunlight, through the slats of our eyes. We are naturally raw with this new-found knowledge, and a bit unhinged. One of us has a temper. The other has a gun.

So-Called

Today, Porous believes what is real grows more boring, as when a tree is just a tree, he says.

I can change my belief tomorrow, he says, but today what is real, so-called, becomes more interesting when it is diced by belief. Well, it always is, just ask the dead, like Werner Heisenberg or Paul Bunyon. Yes, big Paul mixing himself into what he sees, taking account, knowing he is part of cut-and-split cordwood to be stacked to dry, part of the very act of hefting-and-stacking. Act and enactment.

Porous says he has seen cordwood stacked, for instance, into a question-mark from oak, a skeleton key from birch, cairns of mixed hardwood, and labia from cherry. A tree-change instead of a sea-change. An exchange of one belief or another. Something more than real. Meta-real, hyper-real, surreal, irreal, take your pick of labels if you must. Something no longer boring, or so Porous believes.

RAVEN

We all drive forward with a blind-spot following, says Porous. That at least is certain. We sense this blind-spot has no kindness or malice and is fixed in place.

When we think of others sometimes we stop, and turn our heads, and the blind-spot backs up with us toward the dead we remember. That they are there!

We see a raven, silent at first.

Because some of our ghosts stay farther back, back in time, to meet them in our own minds, we, too, must back farther into the past.

Around the dead, the ancient and terrible beak-of-message passes with a language we no longer know, this late in human history; but some of the ancient peoples tried to comprehend, some presuming good omen, some assuming evil from the sight and sound: raven.

How to bring these ghosts and ourselves forward? No, says Porous, not the right question.

How to determine if our dead have become cutthroat or not? That's better.

Like the rest of their physical being sunk through the Earth, then atomically dispersed throughout space, the light of their eyes and their eyes, themselves, have fallen to stars;

and because they cannot see, they slash about wildly, making us think of barbed stalks lashed by wind. We sense them this way.

Once our ghosts sense us, our presence fascinates them, and they are becalmed. At that point we can place them in a small curved space as in a bowl set out on a table, one in which we imagine them faceted as ripened blackberries, their drupelets touching each other, waiting for us to pick them up, waiting to facet-mate with us, there between our fingers; but because the dead are hard to swallow, we must return them. Then they fade.

We all drive forward again.

Looking for berries, the raven flies in and out of the fog.

OLD PILLOW & TIME

The feathers under your head keep leaking from
their cloth case. They want to return to the
fowl who tried to fly south for winter, but who
instead wound up slaughtered, plucked, then
eaten. What now, become mawkish, Porous?

You wonder how many feathers make *plump*
and why stitches in the pillowcase decide to
become undone. "Just average wear and tear,"
you think. But what is "average" to a stitch?
What is a stitch in time? Is this how loneliness
thinks?

Why does an hour before daylight feel longer
than an hour before sunset? What did the
sexagismal Sumerian clock mean by "60?" It's
still dark, so you turn on the night table lamp,
rise and become the shadow cast from the
gnomon of the Egyptian obelisk.

Wait a minute, who is speaking inside this
poem? What is meant by "who?" What is meant
by "minute?"

You stand barefoot on the worn and split
floorboards which hold you even though all of
their sap dried out years ago. You bow down to
your sandals and see tiny pyramids of sand. All
the nails hammered into floorboards are keeping
their heads down, too, for these wooden dead
are flat and strong, not like the tufted dunes in
the dream of the desert panther. More like the
Paleolithic tiger's bones in a museum, or your

house which stands every day in the weather, cloyingly hot like a tomb. If you carve the mask of a god it may become you. Give it time.

Oso

A poem is never finished, only abandoned.
                    —Paul Valery

This time of year again—absurd lawns, weeds
with a buzz cut, newest dandelions beheaded
and their edible greens slashed to the ground,
says Porous.

In a town forewarned a cliffside's sloppled by
rain, people buried in mud, more a brown
avalanche, one more in a world sliding to death,
whole families lost.

A few half-buried houses standing up in muck—
their roofs inverted ship prows about to sink
down with the rest. A home is never finished,
only abandoned. The village philosopher, in his
grief, nevertheless can't stop laughing.

"When Hippocrates arrived, however, he soon
discovered that Democritus was saner than his
fellow citizens. For he alone had recognized
the absurdity of human existence, and was
therefore entirely justified in laughing at it. . . ."

In Oso, dandelions return with a vengeance.

DEFLAGRATION, A FAIRY TALE

Porous told me that Cole, a teenager, lived with his parents in a woodstove the year he began turning orange and blue and then leaping.

"You're a sputterer, too," said his mother on her bed of old ashes.

Big log father didn't like his son's constant flare-ups and inconsistencies, never mind the color of his spikes, so he rolled to one side of the bed, a seethe of anger inside him.

"See," said the mother, "our son's managed to divide us in our bed."

"He conceived this happening; it's another form of splitting," said the father.

"You think that our son conceived us?" said the mother, slightly peeved at the implications.

"Yes," said the father, "he planned the whole fucking thing!"

"I was sure it was the other way around, dear, because he is our son."

The son kept leaping up, leaping up, higher and higher, until both of his parents became angry then angrier, bright orange and a little blue, like him.

Well, of course the parents got really burnt up, but as they did so they found themselves rolling together again in bed, falling into one another as their souls went up the chimney and their ashen bodies became a new bed.

Cole, of course, had momentarily matured. "No more leaping for now," he said, as he sunk down into his parents' bed that was his parents, and glowed there awhile, until he fell asleep.

When we found him we stirred him up. He had been dreaming of new parents. "Here you are, Cole," "meet Cherry and Birch."

"Yes, I was just conceiving them," said Cole, "thank you for bringing them!" and he began to leap.

AFTER LISTENING
TO MORE RADIO NEWS
OF THE DETERIORATING WORLD,
POROUS GOES OUTSIDE
AFTER AN ICE STORM

Between the iced lower branches of this spruce
and the top of this green iron chair left out in
the wind, there's a slim crystalline bridge —sun
on the ice.

I hear snow crashing from pitched roofs.

Our days stiffen with news of a darkness
beyond winter's—little green and connected
may survive.

A desperate boy and his father push through
ash-clogged air as they tramp the road, then a
bridge, barely feeling hope.

I bring them closer, closer, all the time
closer.

Fourth stanza is a reference to Cormac
McCarthy's apocalyptic novel, *The Road.*

Soft Water

Collecting around rock and branch, snow at the edge of the field becomes white stags. Wind swirls and these deer blow back and forth across the road, something Porous in plain sight.

Under tomorrow's sun they will melt into cornstalk stubble and furrows, then seep into old paths and channels—fluid deer collecting in pipes below soil. . . .

During your morning indoor shower their nuzzlings through the hand-held nozzle will connect with your face—stronger and stronger until water flows deer. Wild hair at the drain! Refreshed hide. No noise after a while. Just their eyes above a blue towel. Porous stays inside.

VALENTINE

No wind can stand not to bump into something.
A starving wind chases cardboard boxes down
the road. Even winds crossing deserts strive for
an upright bit of cactus or camel, while wind
over waves makes of the waves lewd motions
and spit, and dunes take the shape of what
wind occurs to them. Sand spits.

No wind fasts long, and the one last night rattled
our dreams like hunger while birds snugged
against wind rehearsed each their own song
as they slept; then we woke with each other
at dawn with their voices the same wind-song
we'd heard when inner winds were first shaping
us and turning our hearts toward each other.

EARTH DAY, POROUS SAYS, IS. . .

when on a fern's crozier there's a splat of birdshit
shaped as a bishop. . .
when a bunting flies over the basil there must
be a poem occurring. . .
when windows feel glare the mare lies down in
the meadow. . .
when things sing all-at-once it must be April. . .
when we love even the air thinks everything is
more. .
when the sun is not wary of sizzle. . .
when a voyeur in a tulip collects until rain. . .
when zig-zag insects become corybantic
dancers. . .
when we savor what is simply there. . .
when the scape is horizoned between sacred
and profane. . .
when shadows migrate from sorrows. . .
when ideals are pry-bars under rainbows. . .
when earth remembers itself and yields what is
above it. . .
when we refuse to accept beautifully appointed
doom. . .
when such a day teaches to turn our caves
inside out. . .
when such a day teaches how to praise and
cure. . .
when this day teaches we are arable and raised.

In Sedona (Etc.)

for Pam (with Brian and Elizabeth)

Climb red rock pine juniper trail with cactus
more than blue spring desert blooms, breezes
in all wending…javelina-nibbled Prickly Pear. .
.pebbles spill under foot…no glam or sooth or
spirit-loiter at vortex…it's only rock and roll…
pick up ancient   magma lot…"Supernova"
glyph on cliffrock "has been determined…"
prehistoric faces drawn child-simple as proto-
emoticons…cropless ancient desert farm…not
much depends upon a red real sparrow…

Clamber in air-fury to peak in a surround of
rock and get a jones for flying from…. Wind
'volumizing' hair….

Hike back to lowest sandstone-scrub-pine-
swift-damp-air-parking-lot where you bargain
with an Apache grouch woman for an Apache-
carved barrette (with mini bear claws incised
in its silver.) Just watching you is love about us
all. Just watching her we load no quarrel.

What crosses all as we leave, I swear, is the
same outlaw wind without alibi for where it
used to breeze.

ALIBI

As Porous tells it: In a canyon, a sound was very hungry, as hungry as a mountain lion, so it went looking for ears.

Finding no ears among the canyon walls, the sound didn't know it was also an echo. In fact, it didn't know what sort of sound it was at all. It lived in hope of more, it shifted in the drift of again.

All echo could do was to hope while feeling its waves growing shorter and shorter in the shadowy air, in the starve of its search, in the bounce from rock, until echo began to decay in its hunger.

Echo, barely existing now, felt the canyon walls touch back with all their history of silence and sun and rain and wind, almost as a friend.

Within the last of its waves echo understood for the first time that hope is a fling with weathers, and that beyond hope there is only rock, that momentary alibi for sound ever unable to tell the origin of.

The Bright Thing

A woman is slowly driving a glass chandelier
on a flatbed truck through the desert, and the
bright thing's shaking all over, its glass beads
like hundreds of tiny testicles warming up.

Don't be afraid, says the woman speaking
through the sliding window of the cab, we're
just going to see how hot you can be in sunlight
and if you can pass your reflections along.

Now we'll stop and make love, says the woman.
and she pulls to a stop and climbs up onto the
bed.

We'll make such a wonderful child, one who
can hang with you while I clean its face and all.
Part flesh and part glass, we can call it Partly. It
will be so bright and obedient with its skin lit
from the inside and my fingers on the dimmer
switch, as you know, dear.

ELEGY

Rain constant rain. It is like certain failings, the vertical ones that come when I have been too ambitious, climbing the syntax of my desire only to find, in the end, I reached too high in my abilities which were then thrown down to earth drop by drop, and hard! I became very dry, an old dog collar left dangling on a hook in a shed.

Rain constant rain. Yet certain plants have urgencies: Ajuga, Rhododendron, and Japanese Iris bloom, and the dogwood tree, a Kousa, blossoms its creamy snow of petals under which a few bones have started up through the soil. Something rises with them, something so alone it cannot easily enter this world.

Rain constant rain. Black weather. In this air there is a thickness as of fur, and I sense a door opening where there is no door, a sense of something roaming, as if light tries to shed from a dark place to golden itself more, as if the air somehow remembers sunlight as a dog making another dog squint.

Rain constant rain. At times indoors I feel an urgency in this house, a sense of animal walls trembling, as if I were holding in my arms again the last shudder of our dying dog, returning now, happier, shot with sunlight through and through, no collar, her ears up...listening into the hallways of her own heart.

See-Saw

1.

Mud. The muck of acts among children, their murky pacts. *You be the queen and I'll be the king.* All is Porous.

And when has there not been a time of politics? Same playground, different see-saws.

Did you say hee-haw?

Say what you will of repetitions and complexities, but it still comes down to a-rebel-touching-the-ground-shoves-up-and-a-dictator-comes-down.

2.

You hold onto the handle while you sit at your end of the see-saw. Nothing sits up in the air at the other end. You shove up, weeee! Nothing goes down. Proof that it is there.

What is meant by "proof?" asks Porous.

Meaning is a form of inadvertent larceny—one steals from things-as-they-seem in order to find a currency for things-as-they-are-believed-to-be.

Porous As The Ancient One

for Harvey and Adrianne Robins

Inside every bear there is an ancient ear listening for the footfalls of man as he moved to untangle broken branches and brush and drag them off to a burn-pile. One man is doing this right now. One bear is listening.

Among those enmeshed limbs in the forest there used to be ease, honey, and a den.

The man goes into his house and takes down an old, sun-faded photograph from a wall. It shows the forest as it once was. He sets the photograph on a table. He tells his wife that he now senses what is left for the bear is like that white shadow left where the photograph had been. The man and his wife hold a sad, new understanding. The man takes down their wedding photograph, too, to see what is left.

They go outdoors and climb up, into their tree-house. There must be some branches missing since there is now a large swatch of sunlight on the floor. How long until rock-a-bye? Soon it will be winter.

They get down on all fours. They curl up together, trying to fill the passing sunlight with their bodies, like children, and take a long, long nap.

Myth Of Ferns

Ferns sprang up and, dried of dew, flounced in
the light. They waved to each other. They were
happy to be, these green women, says Porous.

Men came tramping, stepped on the women,
bruising them, sometimes breaking their stipes,
killing some. Then the men left.

Most of the women got up again and touched
each other with their fronds. No one could
hear them mourning.

A few ferns began to wear yellow-jackets every
morning when men started to walk. The dew
didn't give an ounce, one way or another.

Stung, men began to keep their distance from
the women. Men appeared to darken and look
vertically streaked, even desperate. They were
filling up with rain.

Not far off from the men there were songs in the
air, bouncy ones, like those at a wedding party.
While the men stood in their own storms.

The women rose up and called each other by
name: Polypody; Deer; Royal; Adder's Tongue;
Wood; Spleenwort; and Maidenhead.

Yes, the women rose up in sunlight and waved
to each other again. Not one invited the men to
dance, much less to flounce, not with all that
rain inside them.

Shift Thing, An Assay

Rain glistens in the flashlight's beam: (hid) (den) (fro) (gs).

You who turned on the flashlight may believe
that the haiku monostich above is complete and
real, the light-in-the-dark flashing into strands
of rain, into water from no sky you can see,
though you believe it is there as much as the
two frogs' eyes you seem to see, says Porous.

You believe things exist as they are, and believe
you cannot yet see other things that exist,
therefore you imagine them and make them
'ring true', whether profound or bling, or simply
the frogs you believe you heard and so walked
toward them. Thus comes a universe very soon.

But the real thing, all that is real, is always at
least partly a drafty, shifty, get-my-drift, daffy
alembic grab-bag, wifty and makeshift. Or so I
believe. And so you may believe.

To 'make' sense. What of that? To believe
any world rhymes, say, in verticals, oracles,
miracles, coracles...make any list or just believe
in these sentences right here, yes, the ones you
may be reading; oh yes, believe, as just now the
perhaps sun with its early beams on toy frogs in
a yard, a sum you believe in, comes, comes why,
or merely, like you waking in bed, comes to. . . .

Quotes, A Collaged Letter*

to a fellow poet [add your name]

Dear—

One of the strange things about poets is the way they keep warm by writing to one another all over the world. . . . A correspondence is poetry enlarged. There are two worlds—nature and the post office. When I speak to you of me, I speak to you of you. From lightest words sometimes the direst quarrel springs. I have never known anyone worth a damn who wasn't irascible. ARE MY EARS ON WRONG? Every day we're wrong about something. The soul of another is a dark forest. And then I think that unless one is oneself one cannot do anything much for others. With the best will in the world and even with a great deal of effort, one will always to a certain extent give them stones instead of bread—and both sides know it. Truth today is not truth tomorrow. There's always next year, until there's not. I don't think we would need to take our shoes off to count them. I think there's a kind of desperate hope built into poetry now that one really wants, hopelessly, to save the world. One is trying to say everything that can be said for the things that one loves while there's still time. Fail. Fail again. Fail better. Please excuse my long letter, I didn't have time to write a short one. A quotation is not an excerpt. A quotation is a cicada.

*index for quotations at end of manuscript.

YOGA

Porous flatly states, You might say it is silly
when I say I've been unfair to the katydids at
the end of summer: I've been imposing the
words *plaintive* and *lament* on the sounds of
these wing-scratchers, who took the path of
cryptic shape and coloration, to blend with
green leaves.

It is dusk; just listen.

You are hearing them as they sing and hear
each other as they sing and hear each other as
they sing and hear each other with ears located
near their knees!

It is night; just listen.

You might say it is silly when I say I'll go to bed
with my wife, who can bend and place her ears
just so, while I am still learning to be flexible.
Don't look or listen.

It is night; and it listens.

ORIGIN

This is the way you can know, says Porous:

feel Presences within the land. . .shifting
within the interplays of things with the
animate Earth—how first powers strove out
of Desire, their need a kind of singing within
lack, a perhaps smell of light among stones. No
reverence, but a deference among things, each
with each, as they felt themselves being beings
aligning, powering out the two life-strains:
Vicious-beauty and Fierce-gentleness—dove-
tailing desires!

City Mice; Country Mice

While some we know have that speech- rattle
and blare of urban talk from the very sprockets
of self-snitch and gossip pockets *If you put truth
into the river after a lie, the truth will catch up.*

We know when what is quiet in us speaks it
speaks in being quiet. It speaks in being,
making us listen, making us so quiet we come
closer. So much closer. This close. And we
touch.

S-Box

Don't hinder my lurch, demands Porous, wait until I finish toting this suggestion-box to my office. It feels chock full and it's still locked. I'm certain it contains small stones painted to resemble eyeballs. Some of them will look assertive as if asking for a raise. Most will no doubt look sheepish. When I open the box and take all stones out and place them side-by-side on the conference table, they will resemble certain pebbles found on beaches by the sea, in this case the sea of enmity, roiled by Hot-and-Bothered holding a fund to my head, wanting to roll with more sick time and childcare benefits, you know, et cetera. I'll tell you right now, what I'm going to do is spread the eye-stones on the floor and then set a boulder on top of them. It will resemble an emperor on cobbles, bolder despite the lack of clothes, unless you have another suggestion.

Under Noon Sun

A woman's shadow shrank until it vanished into a colony of ants, Porous tells me, where it blended in perfectly. It emerged from time to time, piecemeal on the backs of ants feeling their way toward an ideal: less like a crumb than a sphere.

Inside the house, the woman knew not to be captious toward an ant spanking an apricot with its antennae; and she knew not to pinch that other ant, that small one waving at her from the umbo of an orange; otherwise, her shadow might never return to her intact. It might never be able to report about those ovoids climbed and tested by the ants.

Later in the day, the woman reported what she had seen to her husband who had been working outside. He felt embarrassed, a little guilty. He confessed that he had eaten the apricot and orange and could not swear that either hadn't even the tiniest bit of shadow on it.

"How was I supposed to know?" asked the husband, sounding irritated now. "What happens if someone eats bits of another's shadow?"

Hearing those questions, the woman felt distraught in her uncertainty. Her husband already seemed changed somehow, slightly depressed, and his skin appeared to be a little darker. She began to believe that her husband had, indeed, swallowed bits of her shadow; but she remembered reading one day that belief without doubt is just credulity.

So, the next day, before noon, the woman went outside to stand under the sun and observe, if she could, her own gnawed shadow, or its lack.

This Poem Wants To Be

a gymnast who somersaults from a balance-
beam, but never lands; instead she *becomes* that
somersault. After a time, someone in her group
asks the somersault to land, please, but the
somersault only spins faster, faster and faster. It
has taken on a life of its own, dissociated.

Now someone holds a rod vertically under the
somersault and says that, together, they make
a pinwheel; and it turns out that the person
holding the rod says she's the gymnast watching
her own somersault spinning above her while
the balance-beam disappears.

It is such a difficult thing, the thing they do,
gymnast and somersault, the vertical and the
round, in a state first learned when the gymnast
was a little girl and her father did unspeakable
things.

INANIMATE DESIRE

The orange kite goes skimming over the sea,
comes in over the sand, then dips closer to the
largest shell, pauses, lifts again and again dips
until the kite hears wind-colored-by-the-sea in
the shell call out to it, this paper sail that can
dance on air. It doesn't have to mean anything.
Joy doesn't prepare. A kite can leap like fire or
fall flat. It doesn't tire. Life is less about meaning
than it is about desire.

PAGAN

At times white hands grope to hold back ocean
waves rushing up and ahead, their falls of foam
headed sand-ward, says Porous. And the moon,
unable to stop them is in such pain that they—
the waves—know not what they do, while
moon—responsible moon—gives its own hands
that each wave may be forgiven its haste in its
rising to death.

Krummholz*

A murder of crows perched on stunted wind-blown pines on a mountain is inside the man day-dreaming on an idiocy of pillows. The pitch of the murder in sunlight.

The day-dreaming man also sees, in the air, two ramshackle shacks, one with an open, unhinged door, the other with a door shut tight. It is the same shack and has the same door all-at-once, but it appears as two, then one, then two, etc. The man is that shack, his day-dreaming tells him. An open man, a closed man, in need of repair.

Shack-and-door is Porous' doppelganger? There have been many cases of doppelgängers appearing to well-known figures: John Donne; Percy Shelley; Guy de Maupassant; even Queen Elizabeth the First, to name a few, but none as a shack with an open and shut door at the same time.

Can symbols be doppelgängers as much as doppelgängers be omens? If there's a 'missing link' cannot there also be a missing gap?

Crows fly in and out of gaps, why not humans? Can we meet in the air and link with our double there?

Porous knew that if he continued this day-dream it would stunt his growth or even make doppelgänger-sooth to death. He grew tired,

hypnogogic, yawned until his pillows allowed
an intelligence of actual dreams.

*Krummholz, the word means stunted
windblown trees growing near the tree line on
mountains.

Something Else

Losing a good-luck charm does not mean losing good luck or that bad luck will occur more frequently. That is why Husband looked into the pickle jar, with its lone occupant. Husband thought that if he could remove the lid, after years of having the jar tightly sealed away in the dark, good luck might befall him in a charming, if not charmed, way.

"My view is kind of difficult to explain," said Husband to Wife.

"It's a belief, that's why," said Wife. Good luck with it.

Husband and Wife stood in the root cellar as Husband held the pickle-in-its-jar to the dim light of a 20-watt bulb.

"I believe the pickle is still in there, dear, said Husband."

"Yes, I believe he's there, too," said Wife, "though the jar is so cloudy."

"Let's call him Something Else," said Husband.

"That won't change the fact that he's still our pickle in the clouds," said Wife.

"No, I suppose not," said Husband, and he placed the boy-in-the-brine back on the shelf, and turned off the light.

NOTHING LIVES IN A THIMBLE

Porous, I have been trying to sleep inside this miniature hat that is really my grandfather's thimble; but the pent up anger of the unrolled keeps me awake. Let me explain. A bolt of cloth has been showing signs of unrolling (if not unraveling.) Yes, I see it now, the bolt beginning to roll itself out, an angry red carpet that begins to scream. My grandfather intervenes, starts cutting the cloth until the bolt's anger becomes so diminished it seeps into space. If I know grandfather he figures God won't mind a seep of anger into space. Grandfather knows God is an atheist like himself, and since grandfather is unassuming, he can't be sure if God reaps what he sews for himself or just sells it to the nearest believer. Grandfather takes up needle and thread, then notices me in his thimble. You have to get out of my thimble, he says. I am respectful, obedient; I climb out onto the now placid red carpet. Grandfather puts the tiny hat on his thumb and begins to sew me, like a decorative fleur-de-lis, onto the red cloth. He calls me Lily and since his needle only tickles, I laugh. Grandfather looks at his thimble, takes it from his thumb, looks into it, into the empty space within, and he says, *Nothing lives in a thimble and between stars, but you can sew with it.*

LIGHT ANGEL

*Angels are the powers hidden in the faculties and
organs of men.—Aristotle*

And when the world began to itch, Glory
scratched its fleas into existence.

Maybe baby, says Porous.

A gloriole of glad sunlight did its best to be born
smack for the muddle of us? No dice?

Who can know? asks Porous.

Tell me from what distant night did a sonnet
scrawl skies, with Shakespeare its light?

DARK ANGEL

Out of sky-lot and wind-blow what devil freights
our roof, and why my compulsion to embody
such force of air and light now as a lucifer of
wind-shear that once attenuated will allow firs to
release birds lucidly?—oh, must be this morning
I have most devilish need, eh Porous?

APPARITIONAL

*after reading about yet another teen-ager's
accidental death*

Listening with earbuds, no aggro in her walk, a
risible disposition, nothing diffident about her
living inside light—she turns and shouts *Sing
while you twerk & you just get more*, as everyone
glues joy of work with bliss of leisure, making
them stick for lots of years already, while some
cockamamie okey-dokey goes a long way
toward unhampering the barriers so that

each heart tips the others
for dying this young.

THE PARTY ALWAYS WINDS UP IN THE KITCHEN

In some households the kitchen winds up in the party, says Porous. People keep wanting more at such times, you know, refills, bits of this, bites of that, until pretty soon a drunk gnaws on a box, another starts eating the cupboards, the refrigerator offers its empty shelves and crispers, the booze is gone, so people chomp on ice, legs of chairs and tables are licked, and soon enough the door handles are gone and no one can figure out how to leave, even through windows. Although glass is a liquid, the windows won't melt fast enough to drink. A sprig of forsythia and a tuba are necking near the doorway. Then through hall-sways and without map, Homunculus enters the capital of reeling, the kitchen, his exuberance of character creating thoughtless expression: a demented whoop, as he finds the host in a missionary position, passed out. Everyone else is in a stupor, and they stare, like cannibals, at the littlest one now among them.

DECONSTRUCTIONIST

Porous tells me the haystacks are assembling in the auditorium. They have been up all night drinking and have barely made it to class this morning. . . just ask professor Dilbert who resembles a pitchfork in this auditorium, so thin and stiff, his three strands of hair standing up like tines. He begins his lecture on Deconstruction. As the professor drones on the brightest haystack begins to understand the tiny glimmer inside her is nothing more than the proverbial needle finding its haystack; but as pointed as it is, in this case the needle only points to itself. Trouble is, the student doesn't want to disassemble for the sake of a needle, especially not her own. And yes, she really thinks a hand out of the universe will come to pick each of us up and toggle each of us until each becomes a black hole with one hand clapping on the other side with nothing, aside from that needle, certain, so certainly yes she thinks yes certainly yes she and ya'll will get the clap.

REGARDING SCISSORS

A pair of scissors wants to approach a Möbius strip and sever it from it, says Porous.

That would be an act of aggression against Infinity, thought the astronomer. Scissors enact with momentary time the desire to touch Infinity so deeply it would become divided from itself; but Infinity long ago left temporal matters to their own devices; and besides, as soon as any manifestation of tick and tock flashes up, scissors or no scissors, Infinity swallows it whole.

The astronomer pondered further. . .

Any attempt to sever Infinity is incomprehensible. It cannot be cut from itself.

Any scissors needs a hand, whose hand who knows? But a hand is key: it has no sense of time on its own and it holds what it can; and it is rumored that August Ferdinand Möbius himself, holding scissors, cut himself, once.

GRAVITY

In a dark room the planet balls of an orrery
arranging themselves differently—we shift
and rearrange ourselves. We drift off to sleep,
we say, while our bodies remain in the place
where they were before we were taken into an
elsewhere or nowhere of sleep, that universe,
a drifting within something we experience as
dream first, then slow waking, then here, where
we orbit, like something we might know.

HOOKED

Miles from me, a woman walks into her own
house as I walk into mine, says Porous. I can hear
her in my head: *We are still arm-in-arm, how long
may I keep your arm?* She's got it all wrong. It
is not my arm she's hooked, but that of the ape
next door to me, the one with whom she was in
love. Now I must listen to the most awful screams
from the ape in pain, and I wonder if anyone will
attend to his bloody arm socket or if he will at
least find a new girlfriend. Not likely. He certainly
wouldn't let me near him, in any case. Plus, he is
now more dangerous than ever: the next lethal
virus is already spilling from animals. It is passed
from arm to arm.

SQUEEZE-BOX

That a caterpillar may sleep with a Slinky is one thing, but it's quite another the way an accordion sleeps with a staircase. All staircases are jealous of accordions; whereas the Slinky was invented as an homage to caterpillars. Their common denominator is the escalator, that metal monstrance commonly of airports, rigid cousin to the Slinky, crushing to caterpillars, and yet each stationary platform moves in a way that suggests caterpillars, accordions, and a medieval torture potential for toes. The latter is why one platform step of the escalator is often heard muttering to another, *Go ahead, punk, ramify my alibi, swivet and sweat your grease.* For these reasons, there are people who fear stepping on and off escalators, especially Lepidopterists, Squeeze-box players, and children with soft shoes, while the handrails keep returning fingerprints and viruses. Here is a serial killer and there is the flu. What you can carry will fly, too.

Tv Screen [Closed Captioned]

We're mostly de-furred these days and there aren't enough fig leaves, if needed, says Porous. We incurred that path of first animals still briny from the sea; later the Biblical big wrath; still later that burning bush just some brush with the so-called law. [*Thunder rumbles.*] Now we can sit down and stalk a vision under construction, say, a cube capable of curtsy or the irony of dust on a broom handle. [*Urgent creepy organ music.*] Leap from your bar mitzvah and attempt grain bin rescue. [*sirens wailing.*] That fly-off-the-handle tantrum of TV announcer [*rain falling hard*] and then baby smacking her mother eating a French fry [*Should have had a V-8*] and just because these things are simultaneous with an apparently warm park are we in somebody's cinema verité or just some REM sleep lamb languorous wig warm seam as we stir a ceiling fan, that being-with-a-chain pulled to make prowess of a tizzy? [*Helicopter blades thwacking closer and closer.*] Step up to the bar. Where are the oneirologists now that we need them? [*Under closed eyelids eyes still tremble.*] Tonight, all links are on them, very few on the house. [*A banquet of cuckoo-clocks eating time, a gala ring of birds at the brink of ruckus.*] Alarmed for awake, now we are deferred, offers Porous.

B.S.

being a little distraction for Ken Koppel on his birthday

Bergie Seltzer threw so much wet spaghetti onto a wall in her apartment, and then glued tiny colored balls, pieces of brightly-colored paper, parts of dolls, colored push-pins, and splattered a few tomatoes and sometimes smashed fruit onto the wall she called "daddy iceberg" in her apartment that summer, that the wall was transformed into a colorful, textured rectangle of mainly organic and drying things.

Bergie signed her initials, B.S., at the bottom of the wall which by fall was suffused with the tints and hues of the discarded and hurled groceries she named, collectively, Arthur, Art for short, says Porous

When a man in a tuxedo showed up, she told him his costume was made of bats and guano, like any critic's, that this peckerhead's taradiddle wouldn't be mistaken for professional assessment since it was only the paradiddle of a woodpecker, and that he had no right to expect marriage even if her bones were perfect and she was able to melt at will or change into anything.

"Pasta on the wall in morning, critics take warning," she said, as she turned into a hallway.

The Artist

All madness aside, says Porous, one is sometimes a porcupine in an unlit cellar full of inflated balloons: how to move naturally according to one's nature, how to proceed at all? Despite the dire proximity of the inflated, to make it to the blackened window and feel impelled to gnaw through its frame to imagined light outside the cellar walls! How the artist tries to tell you s/he is all these things, including the cellar, but can't explain how s/he got there in the first place.

MINIMALIST

study in red

My red is not your red, says Porous. Red as a
light-wave of about 650 nanometers. Blood
as it exits our vessels. Kick-ass red lipstick.
Code Red. Liquid passion to Dracula. Or, well,
molded red Play-Doh of, well, red Plato, else
Orwell. Red men break no treaties. Let us choke
on what red reaches: war, red beaches.

Theatre Star

Real Life

Living constantly in a swarm of crowds creates the star's fixed-in-place smile, gleam of teeth a type of light, says Porous. Of course a scrutiny of mirrors, as if through the eye of a needle another eye looking back. No. More than one. Certain insects come to mind. Also their sounds. Legs rubbing together. Mandibles. To be a blatherskite whose palaver stops only when a cadaver. Some stars begin to resemble, until they become, the one in the last box, the coffin.

The Final Act

There are stars on the ceiling in the funeral home watching the sealed caskets beneath them, says Porous. They look for the "burp valve" on each of the gleaming boxes, but see none. Unseen bodies swell below them. Some stars worry about Exploding Casket Syndrome, but soon realize that, for ceiling stars, that is silliness redux. A balloon full of water is not afraid to pop. Let others below clean up. No one tells the families. [Off stage: the sound of a dial spinning this way and that and this, a safe being opened and shut.]

Question from a fan: What is angel wing-pitch?

Their wing-pitch is the angle of the wings compared to the horizontal, the corpse. Quality angels have a wing pitch of 12-14 degrees. Lesser angels can have a wing pitch as low as 8-10 degrees. The higher the pitch, the more pressure the angel applies to the air in front of it as it turns and the more air is forced downward. That is why some lesser quality angels can look like they're spinning up a storm, but when you stand under them, you cannot feel anything. The best way to judge is to test the angel in actual use, but, according to Porous, one must first be horizontal.

Re-Birth, the Curtain Rises

Is that only an artificial haze across the sets, enveloping the stage upon which the future will dance? It swirls toward me in this darkened theatre and I sense an audience of ghosts, a collective past to which I'm present enough to hear its shifts as the gray continues from no visible source—no one yet in the wings. . . .

THE AWARD

Whoever wins, says Porous, will be represented
by cotton candy at the lips of a child licking at
the carnival after that sticky fluff's presented over
scattered sacred books:

Analects of Confucius / *Bhagavad Gita* / *Upanishads*
/ *Tao Te Ching* / *Buddhist Sutras* / *Tibetan Book of
the Dead* / *Egyptian Book of the Dead* / *Torah* / *New
Testament* / *Quran* / with the unsacred *Gilgamesh*
suddenly tearing out their pages and *Enkidu* the
hairy wild man flooding them with each other
until they resolve into a single swallow

of candy under lights.

CABINETS

Most people have indentations on the top of their head, something for an alien screwdriver to fit, says Porous. Feel for yourself. Easiest for the hairless ones. We are all being turned clockwise all the time. The infant is held up to be admired or simply because it stinks, its parents turning it around, turning it over and around. Later, kids watch clocks and days and toys turn around. Adolescents sense themselves turning and becoming dizzy. Then everyone slows down in middle-age, but we keep on being turned. The oldest people are turning dizzy with more frequency. Gravity-and-time makes one alien screwdriver. Once in a while you can feel it on the top of your head the way the board of a cabinet can sense a cabinet-maker screwing it down. Can it? Can you? So many boards, each carefully measured, sanded, planed and fitted by experience. Trouble is, there is no cabinet-maker. There are only cabinets being screwed. *What uselessness!* you may cry. Perhaps. It depends upon the type of wood being used. It depends upon what you have in your drawers. Anything meaningful? At last, most cabinets are placed inside larger cabinets that are placed inside the earth, the earth with gravity-and-time, the earth which never stops turning because it, too, is being screwed.

THRENODY: LAST FREE HAND

The twins thought they heard some strange and some familiar voices in their sleep. When they woke the next morning the house was full of people who were silent and looked away from them. They found their aunt in the kitchen and she asked them to sit down, she had something to tell them. She told them their mother had disappeared. "Yeah, sure" the twin 10 year olds said together. But the aunt explained that their mother had died holding onto the handrail as she descended the eight steps from one upstairs landing to another last night after tucking them into their bunk beds. She died holding onto the rail they all used to pretend went all the way to the sea. "She had water in her lungs, pneumonia," said their aunt and then vanished inside her own voice while the boys were wiping tears from their eyes.

Where is this going? asks Porous.

Since the twins and their mother did live by the sea, the next day the boys unscrewed the metal clasps holding the wooden handrail, really a thick six-foot wooden dowel, and brought it outdoors. They each carried one end of the handrail and marched into the water, then slogged further through low tide, the handrail still firmly in their grips. They sunk one end of the handrail at a 45° angle into the underwater sand then held on and waited until the tide grew higher and higher. They were in the water a long time, sometimes choking from the slap of a surprise wave.

Their aunt, who could not swim, came outside and was frantically waving her hands and yelling something from the shore, said Porous, just as the boys began the long descent to their mother, each boy waving back with his last free hand.

Mug Shot

Lashed to a sugar cube, looking for coffee in my mug, I have on my anti-scald wet suit and teaspoon-shaped flippers and gloves. It is pure desire that reduced and placed me on this cube in the first place. When nose and tongue await flavor, it is best that such desire precede the actual occasion of sips. I know to tie myself down, so as not to be jostled and fall off when the cube is dropped.
Every day starts somewhere between geometry and water, says Porous.

I plop into my mug and start stirring swimming. I also add my ego into the mug, let it dissolve, and I sip slowly. There is always a hot way to swallow pride. It is a lot like gulping flippers, gloves, and all.

Scientists say that after liquid is stirred in a vessel at least one molecule returns to its original position once the liquid settles. What about being emotionally 'stirred'? What position does one return to?

As caffeine begins to whirl my nervous system, I sense it as a pinwheel spinning in morning fog, that same fog that lifted off the pillow with me.

Every scintilla of morning is on a need to row basis, says Porous, and adds: gravity and hustle will split their boats.

What to do and how to do all and everything? Behind every door, answers eavesdrop on the deft noise of questions. To sip, perchance to dream. . . .

ENCOUNTER

Jeremiad Inkhorn was full of 'sour grapes' and his breath had the odor of bonnyclabber, according to Porous, who said the man kept on whispering into my ear, his personal space intruding on my own, stifling me, as if some sort of sordid symbiosis was about to happen, and so I stabbed the man on the spot. Some will think that a violent act for such a minor social offense, no doubt, but they will not have seen the devil.

One must think and act quickly in such instances. The man fell to the floor and soon appeared dead. Among the possessions found in his wallet was an N.R.A. membership card, a letter from some far right-wing party official, and a photograph of Adolph Hitler. It is important to understand, also, that he slipped the handle of the knife into my hand, oh, with such urgency.

THE ARCHAEOLOGIST
SPEAKS TO HER INTERN

Even Late Pleistocene human population bottlenecks needed relief. Although most individuals leapt forward, there is evidence that occasionally one jumped from the cliff edge while facing backwards and thus may have watched the rush of rock-face while falling for a new twist of view in that early world.

Ahh, the furred avant-garde, says Porous.

Today, among these remains at the base of the cliff, we'll set the bones of his neck on the ground next to the ossified gossip of jaws, the aegis of ribs, no shadow to the slender arms, just bone jolly absorption tease and other nonsensical things, skull gone to charred granite from the fire pit.

He might have been a first artist listening to the forebears of those wings in the cave behind you, as he was learning to tune the wind with his hair.

He landed flat.

His heart vanished on that stone in your hand.

INDEX FOR SENTENCES IN COLLAGED LETTER

In the order of their appearances:

One of the strange things about poets is the way
they keep warm by writing to one another all over
the world....
—Virgil Thompson

A correspondence is poetry enlarged.
—Robert Duncan

There are two worlds—nature and the post office.
—Henry David Thoreau

When I speak to you of me, I speak to you of you.
—Victor Hugo

From lightest words sometimes the direst quarrel
springs.
—Cato the Elder

I have never known anyone worth a damn who
wasn't irascible.
—Ezra Pound

ARE MY EARS ON WRONG?
—Charles Ives

Every day we're wrong about something.
—Henry Miller

The soul of another is a dark forest.
—Russian saying

And then I think that unless one is oneself one cannot
do anything much for others. With the best will in
the world and even with a great deal of effort, one will
always to a certain extent give them stones instead of
bread—and both sides know it.
—Isak Dinesen

Truth today is not truth tomorrow.
—Claude Chabrol

There's always next year, until there's not. I don't think
we would need to take our shoes off to count them.
—Russell Edson

I think there's a kind of desperate hope built into poetry
now that one really wants, hopelessly, to save the world.
One is trying to say everything that can be said for the
things that one loves while there's still time."
—W.S. Merwin

Fail. Fail again. Fail better.
—Samuel Beckett (*card tacked to the wall beside his desk*)

Please excuse my long letter, I didn't have time to write
a short one.
—Mark Twain

A quotation is not an excerpt. A quotation is a cicada.
—Osip Mandelstam

DAVID GIANNINI's most recently published collections of poetry include *Faces Somewhere Wild* (Dos Madres Press,) *Span Of Thread* (Cervena Barva Press,) *Az Two* (Adastra Press,) a "Featured Book" in the 2009 Massachusetts Poetry Festival; and *Rim/*Wave (Quale Press.) 14 of his chapbooks were published 2013-17 including *Inverse Mirror*, a collaboration with artist, Judith Koppel;. His work appears in national and international literary magazines and anthologies. He was nominated for a Pushcart Prize in 2015. Awards include: Massachusetts Artists Fellowship Awards; The Osa and Lee Mays Award For Poetry; an award for prosepoetry from the University of Florida; and a 2009 Finalist Award from the Naugatuck Review. He has been a gravedigger; beekeeper; taught at Williams College, The University of Massachusetts, and Berkshire Community College, as well as preschoolers and high school students, among others. Giannini was the Lead Rehabilitation Counselor for Compass Center, which he co-founded as the first rehabilitation clubhouse for severely and chronically mentally ill adults in the northwest corner of Connecticut. www.davidgiannini.com

Made in the USA
Columbia, SC
06 May 2017